Massage

& Meditation

George Downing

illustrated by Anne Kent Rush

A RANDOM HOUSE • BOOKWORKS BOOK

First printing, February 1974,   1,500 copies in cloth
                                 25,000 copies in paperback
Second printing, April, 1974,   15,000 copies in paperback
Third printing, December, 1980,   3,500 copies in paperback

Cover design and illustrations by Anne Kent Rush
Typeset by Vera Allen Composition Service, Hayward,
    California (special thanks to Dorothy and Irene)

This book is co-published by   Random House Inc.
                                201 East 50th St.
                                New York, N.Y. 10022

                        and   The Bookworks

Distributed in the United States by Random House, and
simultaneously published in Canada by Random House of
Canada Limited, Toronto.

LIBRARY OF CONGRESS CATALOGING IN
PUBLICATION DATA

Downing, George.
Massage & meditation.

"A Random House/Bookworks book."
1. Massage.   2. Meditation.   I. Title.
RM721.D63   615'.822   73-20585
ISBN 0-394-49237-4
ISBN 0-394-70648-X (pbk.)

Manufactured in the United States of America

CONTENTS

*Thanks to Carole and to Don
for their enthusiasm and support.*

A NEW STEP

This book's title, and hence its purpose, may surprise you. Massage *and* meditation? What's the "and" doing here? Isn't massage interpersonal, accomplished by actions and movements, and practiced with one's attention focused upon another person instead of upon oneself? And isn't meditation totally private, something done with complete physical stillness, and in an inner darkness behind closed eyelids? Aren't these two completely unrelated disciplines? Two different universes? Not in the least.

This book's point of view is, on the contrary, that massage and meditation are in key aspects very much alike. Beyond that, the two activities can be put together in ways which give new depth to both. And you yourself can begin to experience what it can be to integrate the two. You can do this easily, independently of how much previous experience you have or haven't had with either.

First let's look a little more closely at meditation. Historically speaking, it is neither novel nor outlandish to suggest that meditation and some related discipline might be fused into a

1

single activity. Take for example Japanese zen meditation. Traditionally practiced by sitting perfectly still and focusing inwardly,[1] zen methods of 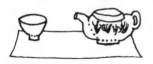 meditation have been a major influence in the East for over a thousand years. Yet during these centuries zen meditation has also been combined with a number of other activities, and these in turn have come to be practiced as distinct meditative forms: calligraphy, flower-arranging, *haiku* composition, and the service of tea, for example. All physical activities these; yet at the same time they have evolved as ceremonies, as ritualistic extensions of meditative principles.[2] Or look at many of the oriental martial arts. Aikaido, Tai Chi Chuan, zen archery, and a number of other Eastern methods of combat are practiced first as meditations and only secondarily as a means of overcoming an opponent.[3] The Japanese zen archer stands with his eyes open, his muscles readied and alive, and his meditative

---

[1] Along with a variety of additional techniques, of course. See for example Phillip Kapleau, ed., *Three Pillars of Zen,* Beacon.

[2] A good introduction to this side of zen is Daisetz T. Sukuki's *Zen and Japanese Culture,* Bollingen.

[3] See for example Eugen Herrigel, *Zen in the Art of Archery,* Vintage.

attention focused equally on the outside target and his own inner being. The Chinese master of Tai Chi even during private meditation moves constantly, never once allowing his body to become totally still. Extending the same meditation when fighting with another, he must at one and the same time tune into the deepest levels of his own nature and "listen with his hands" to the slightest flicker of change in his opponent's movement.

In other words, what we discover when we actually take in the scope and breadth of Eastern tradition is that the practice of meditation has been very effectively combined with other, related physical activities. And that the product of these combinations is often an entirely new meditative form, which in turn develops its own rules, its own tradition, its own history. Over the centuries this has happened a number of different times in a number of different ways. This fact alone might naturally raise for us the question, why not meditation and massage?

Let's turn to the other side and look a little more closely at massage itself. Only now let's look not at what an observer would see from the outside — one person rubbing someone else's muscles — but at the inner experience of the two people involved. Here right away we find something interesting. The popular view of massage[1] is that it

---

[1] I speak of course of legitimate, traditional massage, not what today passes under the same name in most so-called "massage parlors."

is designed to bring about "relaxation." Yet those who have had a lot of familiarity with massage tend to speak differently. They will tell you that when receiving a good massage something more profound takes place in them than "relaxation." My own language for this phenomenon is that I find myself becoming more fully in touch with my aliveness; I feel myself reaching a state of inner expansion, of increased inward contact. Others will use different words, but will point to an experience of a similar nature. Nor is this all. Those who know not only massage, but meditation as well, will report that many aspects of the two kinds of experience are strikingly similar. In other words, the "something more" experienced through massage can feel much like a "something more" experienced through meditation. It is a little as if we were to listen to the same music transposed into two different keys.

Surprisingly enough, much the same can be said about the experience of giving a massage. Naturally there are differences between giving and receiving, between touching and being touched. Yet if we turn again to those who are familiar with massage, we hear that the experience of giving a massage can be, for many, just as rich and varied as that of receiving it. And that its affinities with the experience of meditation are equally similar. So important is this possible intensity of feeling on the part of the giver that in the last decade whole new styles of massage, particularly Esalen massage as developed at Esalen Institute in California, have grown up around it. Whether we happen to be on the giving or receiving end, massage at times has the power to open us to the depths of our being. As simple an act as massage is, there is a mystery at the heart of it. A mystery worth exploring.

It begins to make sense. From the side of meditation it has been possible a number of times in the past to combine its forms and disciplines with those of a related physical activity. And from the side of massage the similarities of inner experience strongly suggest that it might become more closely and more explicitly tied to the practice of meditation. But what comes next? How, practically speaking, might one go about putting the two together? Where to start? What steps to take?

That's what this book is all about. How the two can go together. How you yourself, through a number of practical suggestions and experiments, can begin putting the two disciplines together in your daily life.

This book, I suspect, will play different roles for different readers. Precisely what role it is likely to play for you will probably depend upon how much or little previous experience you have had with meditation and, separately, with massage.

Let me say right away that to use this book you don't need any previous experience with either. If that is your situation then start in right here with massage and meditation both — admittedly an unorthodox way to begin, yet my hunch is you will find it highly effective. A chapter I have included on massage fundamentals, plus the meditations themselves (which make up most of this book) will be enough to get you going. Later, once you have started to feel at home with both forms of practice, you may want to move on to *The Massage Book* in order to pick up additional techniques and also to other, more thorough works on meditation.[1]

On the other hand, if you have already put in some time learning massage, or meditation, or both, then this book will most likely represent for you a continuation of paths you have already begun to explore. If you are already familiar with meditation but not massage, the explorations outlined in the following pages will help you learn how to translate your meditative experience through the medium of touch. If you already know massage but not meditation, then the same set of experiments will not only make your technique itself better, more "on;" they will also give you a much fuller, richer sense of yourself both when giving and when receiving massage. Finally, if neither meditation nor massage are at all new to

---

[1] I particularly recommend Christmas Humphreys, *Concentration And Meditation,* Penguin; Philip Kapleau, ed., *Three Pillars of Zen,* Beacon; Claudio Naranjo and Robert E. Ornstein, *On The Psychology Of Meditation,* Viking; and Shunryu Suzuki, *Zen Mind, Beginner's Mind,* Weatherhill.

you, this book can help you integrate the two in ways which you may never have considered and with results that may surprise you.

For those of you who know *The Massage Book* I might add that what I've tried to do in these pages is to pick up where I left off there. In *The Massage Book* I spelled out a lot of specific techniques for giving a massage, and then also tried to show how massage can have deeper possibilities as a sort of gateway to nonverbal communication between partners and to one's own changing awareness of himself or herself on a bodily level. Here I've gone straight to the second of these, massage as a gateway, and have tried to explain in more practical and explicit terms how this dimension of massage can be tasted, explored, and made a part of one's life.

I've tried to do this in three ways.

First, in the following pages I've described a number of short, meditative experiments which you can use anytime you plan to give a massage. Some are designed to precede the massage, some are for during it and others are for immediately afterwards. All of them can help intensify the inward dimension of your experience while giving a massage.

Second, I've included a number of similar meditations which you can use to heighten your ability to receive a massage. This may sound odd to you — that there can be an art to receiving a massage, and that this art can even be developed and cultivated. Strangely enough, it's true. However powerful your own experience of being massaged may feel to you, there is more that you can learn to let in; much more. Developing your receptivity through meditation will teach you how.

Third, I've added a number of meditations which you and a partner can practice together. These can be used very effectively in combination with the previous meditations. Those for giver and receiver alone will allow each of you to go more fully into yourselves, and the interpersonal meditations which follow can then provide a like means of deepening your contact with each other.

So start in. If massage is totally new to you turn to the chapter on massage fundamentals. Otherwise turn right away to the meditations themselves. More explicit instructions for how to make use of the meditations will be in the same section.

Good traveling.

SOME MASSAGE FUNDAMENTALS

This chapter is for those who are starting from zero. If you have already worked with *The Massage Book,* or have picked up some massage by any other means, then feel free to skip this chapter and turn straight to the meditative exercises that come after. Otherwise I suggest that you start here. Acquaint yourself now with this much of the basics of massage, and you will find that you will be able from the beginning to explore its affinities with meditation.

First the matter of equipment. All you really need is some padding to lay on the floor, and oil. Try padding an inch or two thick — foam is fine — and wide and long enough that the friend you are going to massage can lie down and still leave room for you to sit or kneel to one side. Or use more narrow padding, such as a sleeping bag, along with a comfortable cushion or separate pad for yourself. Don't use a bed unless you have to: it won't provide a firm enough support. A single mattress moved onto the floor will work fairly well, however.

If you discover that you like doing massage,

you may eventually want a padded massage table. I
like a table around thirty inches high, six feet long,
and a little over two feet wide. Information on
how to build a portable wooden table can be found
in *The Massage Book.*

For oil, use any vege-
table oil: olive and sesame
are the easiest to
wash out of sheets
and clothes. Scent
your oil with
something nice smelling, such as musk or cinna-
mon. Or get any of the commercially prepared
massage oils that lately have appeared on the
market.

Pick a place to work that is both warm and
quiet. The temperature must be 70° or over. If
necessary use an extra heater. Or a heating lamp.
Some people who do massage regularly even keep a
heating lamp suspended from the ceiling over the
spot where they work.

So much for arrangements. The next step is
simply to start in, letting your own hands teach
you as you go.

Have your friend that you are going to
massage undress, or else remove whatever amount
of clothing feels comfortable, and lie down. You
can then sit or kneel to one side; or stand, if
working at a table. Another option, when working
on the back, is to sit straddling the backs of your

friend's thighs. Take your time. Settle into yourself. Make sure that you are comfortable.

Next apply the oil, putting about half a teaspoon at a time first into your own palm and then spreading it smoothly over your friend's skin. Cover with a barely visible film of oil the entire surface area of whatever part of the body you have chosen first to massage.

Then start. Begin moving your hands, keeping the full palm in contact with the surface of your friend's body. Your hands are your teachers now; listen to them as carefully as you can.

There are a few things worth exploring right away. One is how to keep your hands relaxed. Most people without realizing it tend to stiffen their hands while they do massage. This cuts down on their sensitivity, makes their movements jerky, and creates unnecessary tiredness in their wrists and arms. Try instead to keep your hands as loose and flexible as you can.

Another is how to apply pressure. Be definite and firm in your movements; without stiffening yourself, lean some of your weight into your hands. Try out different degrees of pressure, checking each time with your friend to find out which feels best to him or her. Most people's bodies are not fragile, and you will probably discover your friend wanting quite a bit more pressure than you had expected.

Another secret concerns the knack of paying attention to the rest of your body while doing massage. This means first of all taking care of yourself by shifting your weight and posture whenever necessary so that you stay as comfortable as possible. It also means allowing the rest of your body to move slightly, in whatever way feels natural, as you move your hands. Think of swaying a little, or of dancing; the movement might be hardly noticeable to an outside observer, but you yourself should be conscious of it. The effect will be both to conserve your strength, and to give a more flowing quality to what your hands are doing.

Most important of all, let yourself experiment with all the different ways of moving your hands that you can think of. Explore, for example, all the ways you can move your palms in long strokes up and down the part of the body you are massaging; ask your friend for feedback as you go, so that you find out what feels best to him or her. Next perhaps take your hands into circles; little ones first, then wide ones. Then begin to let your hands more carefully explore the structure of bone and muscle beneath the skin. Don't worry at this point about formal anatomy, whether you know any or not. Instead just ask your hands: what movements do this softness here, this hardness there suggest? How might this particular set of muscles best be sculptured, articulated, made more definite to its owner?

Explore different rhythms as well; begin to make yourself familiar with the various effects of slow, medium and quick tempos of movement. Also try out ways of using your hands other than with the full palm. Kneading, for example, just as you would do with bread dough. Or using only your fingertips: press them firmly in tiny circles directly against the muscles beneath. Or gentle slapping. Or tapping. Or whatever else occurs to you.

Each part of the body, if you let it, will suggest something new to you. Can you find a way to outline the features of the face? To go in between the toes? To make more precise to its owner the contours of a shoulder blade? Think of your hands and your friend's body as being engaged in a dialogue, and of your own job being to give as much room as possible to let this dialogue take place.

Don't worry, by the way, about the order in which you move from part to part of the body. Start where you like, end where you like. If you decide to work on more than a single part, then apply more oil each time you move to a new area. Try of course to minimize the amount of turning over that your friend has to do. The back, I might add, is an excellent place to experiment with new strokes. Also you will find it easiest to work on the arms, hands, feet, and neck (reaching behind with your palms and fingertips) while your friend is lying face up.

Even more important, don't worry about how much or how little you do. Instead pay attention not to tire yourself. You will be exploring many new ways of moving and positioning your own body, and if you don't take care to pace yourself you will end up with sore muscles. There is also no need right away to try to give a complete massage. Concentrating for now on one or two body parts at a time will do more for both yourself and your friend.

What next? How can you go on from here to learn some more formal massage techniques? Endless numbers of specific techniques do of course exist: some centuries old, others that have been developed during the last decade at growth centers such as Esalen. Once you have really explored on your own what your hands can do, you will later discover yourself picking up more traditional methods with surprising ease. You might start by working through *The Massage Book,* or any other that you find helpful. Or take a class or workshop at a good growth center. Or trade skills with a friend who knows massage. Experimenting first on your own — getting acquainted with your hands as if they were two new friends — is the chief thing. After that, if you find you like massage, acquiring more and more technical knowledge will happen almost by itself.

Finally, don't forget to start experimenting right away, or as close to right away as feels comfortable to you, with the meditative exercises that follow. Of course massage technique has its place, as I would be the last to deny; what you stand to learn from the meditative approach, however, goes beyond all technique. As I said before, what really brings each of us to massage is our longing for contact and for a sense of expanded spaciousness within. Start with that way of looking at it, stay all along with that way of looking at it, and I promise you that massage will treat you well; better and more beautifully than you could ever guess.

HOW TO USE THE MEDITATIONS

The following pages contain detailed descriptions of forty-five meditations. They have been arranged in three sections: the first for the giver of the massage, the second for the receiver, and the last for both together. Within each section are separate meditations for the time prior to, during, and after giving or receiving a massage. The meditations themselves are largely self-explanatory. Read first through the suggestions below, however, and you will find this part of the book a little easier to use.

**Start small. There is no need to try all the meditations at once. Pick one or two that appeal to you, let yourself experiment with them, and return at a later time to some of the others.

**The sequence in which the meditations are presented is not important. If you are trying more than one at a time (i.e., in the period before, or during, or after the same massage), use any order that you wish. With some meditations I have suggested one or another particular combination as especially effective. Feel free, however, to substitute your own sequences and combinations.

**The symbols ~~🖐~~ , ~~🖐~~ , and ~~🖐~~ have been included in order to help you find your way around the different sections more easily. A ~~🖐~~ symbol indicates a meditation intended for the giver of a massage, a ~~🖐~~ one for the receiver, and a ~~🖐~~ one for both together.

**Although interesting, it is not essential that both the giver and receiver of a massage use the meditations. You may use any of them by yourself (except of course those for both partners together), independently of your partner's approach to his or her own experience.

**Vary the amount of time you spend doing any one meditation as much as you wish. Here again I suggest that you start small, taking in the neighborhood of five or less minutes for a single meditation. Then, as the meditations become more familiar, you may lengthen this time as much as fits for you.

**Some of the meditations require that you sit. This you may do most effectively (except in certain cases where indicated) in either of two ways. One is to sit cross-legged on the floor, or if you prefer, on a pillow. The other is to sit on a straight-back chair, knees a couple of feet apart. In either case try to sit comfortably upright, without straining, and, unless otherwise indicated, with your eyes closed.

**This last suggestion is the most important of all. Keep a journal. Write down which meditations you have tried, and your experience each time you tried them. Date your entries and every now and then look back to see where you have been. The longer the period of time that you maintain this record, the more vividly the direction of your own inner development will begin to show itself in its pages.

giver

1

prior

Here is one of the simplest and most basic forms of breath meditation. An excellent meditation in itself, it is also the best possible "warm-up" for any of those which follow.

Sit comfortably. Have your eyes closed. Rest your hands either palms up on your knees or in your lap with the fingers curled lightly upwards. Focus on your abdomen and let your breath flow there, feeling your belly expand with each inhalation and sink back inwards with each exhalation. Allow your breath its own rhythm: don't force it in any way to be large, or to be steady, or to take on any particular rhythmic pattern.

Don't hold your breath once your inhalation is full. After each exhalation, however, try to wait until your breath itself "decides" to return. It may return right away, it may return several seconds or more later; let it tell you what it wants to do. Pay particular attention to the changing length, and to the feel and texture of this natural pause after each exhalation.

If your breath wants to continue upward into your chest, let it do so. Don't surpress any natural movement of your ribs. Just make sure that on each cycle your breath returns to your abdomen, and that the focus of your attention stays anchored there.

That's all. Just follow your breath as if there were nothing else to do. Elementary as it sounds, this is one of the best doors you can open for going inside yourself.

2

A basic meditation for putting yourself more in touch with your hands.

Sit comfortably. For a minute or more focus on the movement of your breath in your abdomen, as in meditation 1. Then hold your hands in the air a little in front of you, several inches apart; turn the palms so that they face each other. Now each time you breathe imagine that your inhalation is going to your abdomen and then that your exhalation is traveling down your arms and into your hands. Pay particular attention to the quality of feeling — physical and emotional — that develops in your hands as you breathe into them.

3

There are a number of ways to take the preceding meditation a step farther. Here's one.

After breathing into your hands for a while, focus more exactly on a spot at the center of each palm. First imagine that your exhalation is leaving your body right at this spot. Then, after a minute or two of this, imagine that a beam of light or energy is now passing back and forth between the two spots.

Let yourself play with this beam, experimenting with moving your hands closer together (don't let them actually touch) and farther apart. Notice at what points your hands seem to want to move even closer together, at what points they want to push apart, and at what points you most strongly feel a sense of connectedness between them.

4

prior

Another continuation of meditation 2.

Make your hands into loose fists. Go on breathing into them, as in meditation 2. Only now, each time that you exhale, open your hands a tiny fraction of an inch. Restraining your hands so that they don't open all at once will feel difficult; try nevertheless to take a number of breaths to let your hands open fully. Then, once they feel comfortably open (without in any way feeling stretched or strained), imagine that with each exhalation they are physically growing a little larger. Continue at the same time, with each exhalation, to let the muscles in your hands move in any minute way that they want.

prior

5

More with your hands.

Hold your hands a little in front of you and breathe into them, as in meditation 2. Now imagine that your hands are getting warmer. That each exhalation leaves them a tiny bit warmer than before. Imagine this as vividly as you can. (If you had the necessary laboratory equipment you would discover that this meditation does literally raise the physical temperature of your hands!)

6

A difficult one, but one of the best for getting more in touch with your hands.

Breathe into your hands, as in meditation 2. Then, when you feel ready, open your eyes and look at your hands. Try not to strain your eyes; don't worry about whether your hands stay sharply in focus. Do, however, try to keep them constantly at the center of your field of vision without glancing away.

At the same time keep silently repeating to yourself, over and over, "This is me." No matter what other thoughts come to you, or what unusual visual phenomena occur, keep coming back to your hands and to this simple affirmation, "This is me."

To do massage really well you need to be as much in touch with the lower part of your body as with your hands. To use the language of bio-energetics, the expressiveness of your gesture towards another depends on how thoroughly your own body is grounded. Here is an experiment based on the work of Magda Proskauer which can help put you more in contact with your pelvis and legs.

Lie on your back. Bring your knees up so that your legs are standing with the soles of the feet on the ground. Have your feet as far apart as the width of your shoulders. Now begin to let your breath flow into your abdomen, as in meditation 1. Remember to let the front wall of your abdomen rise a little as you inhale, sink a little as you exhale. Remember also to look for a natural pause after each exhalation.

After a few minutes add the following movement to the rhythm of your breath. On every other breath as you inhale raise your pelvis a little off the ground, and as you exhale set it gently back down. Don't strain; lifting your tailbone just an inch or two from the ground is fine. Make the movement as smooth as possible, using the full length of your breath to go up and back down. On the in-between breaths just rest, continuing to experience the flow of breath into your pelvis.

8

More for the pelvis and legs.

Stand comfortably. Close your eyes as usual. Have your feet about as far apart as the width of your shoulders. Are your knees locked? If so, loosen them a little.

Now let your breath flow into your pelvis, as in meditation 2.

At the same time imagine that you are loosening all the muscles about the pelvis, as if you could allow muscle and skin to separate a little from the bone; as if you could feel your breath begin gently to flow between the muscles and the bone. Think of the front wall of the abdomen growing softer and softer. Of the buttocks beginning to hang down. Of the pelvic floor — the genitals, the anus, and all the network of small muscles around them — gradually lowering. At the same time imagine the weight of your torso to be passing more and more directly into your legs.

Next shift to one side, so that you are standing on one foot. (Leave the other foot on the ground, but don't put any weight on it.) Continue to think of your breath as both loosening and lowering your pelvis, and at the same time let your weight transmit itself even more directly into the leg on which you are standing. Take your time; pay attention as usual to the quality of the pause after

29

prior

each exhalation. Next, when you feel ready, shift to the other leg and do the same. Then center your weight between the two legs and, paying particular attention to any changes in the feel of space and contour within your pelvis, continue a little while longer as before.

9

This one, which concentrates on the feet, is equally effective by itself or as a continuation of meditation 7.

Lie on your back. Breathe into your pelvis, as in mediation 1. Gradually begin to imagine that your breath is going not only into your pelvis, but also down the length of your right leg. Think of your inhalation as traveling part way down  the leg, and your exhalation as passing right out the sole of your foot.

Then, when you feel ready, add the following movement to the cycle of your breath. On every other breath, as you inhale slowly flex your right foot (i.e., bend at the ankle in such a way that your toes move towards your head). And as you exhale let the foot return to whatever position in which it naturally comes to rest. Move smoothly; don't strain. Rest on the in-between breaths, still breathing down the length of your leg. Flex and release the foot in this manner a half dozen to a dozen times.

Next do the same in the opposite direction. On every other breath extend your foot (i.e., bend

prior

now at the ankle so that your toes point away from you) as you inhale, and let the foot return to a natural resting position as you exhale. Do this also a half dozen to a dozen times.

Go through the same sequence with the other leg and foot. Then, when you feel finished, stand up and see how you now experience the feel of your feet against the ground.

10

prior

More for the feet, and a nice follow up to meditation 9.

Stand comfortably. Let your breath go to your pelvis, as in exercise meditation 1, and then gradually begin to breathe "into" your legs, as in 9. Only now begin to imagine that your breath is going down the length of both legs at once and that your exhalation is going right into the ground itself, leaving each foot at a spot at the center of the sole.

Pay particular attention to the feel of the ground beneath you as you breathe into it. How far, for example, do you find yourself imagining that your breath penetrates into the ground? And what seems to happen to your breath as it enters the ground? Do you imagine it becoming a straight shaft of air? A circulating current? A dissipating mist? What qualities does the ground begin to take on? Alive? Dead? Moving? Stationary? Friendly? Alien? How do these qualities change as you continue the experiment?

Each of us possesses within himself an extremely subtle radar system which can pick up the patterns of tension in other people's bodies. This meditation will help you get more in touch with your own radar.

Sit comfortably. Have your friend stand in front of you some ten to fifteen feet away. Prepare yourself with meditation 1, breathing into your abdomen. Then, when you feel ready, open your eyes and allow them slowly to drift several times without stopping up and down your friend's body. Then close your eyes, picture your friend's body, and try to let swim into your mind an image of yourself in some way healing or otherwise taking care of some part of his or her body. You may see yourself touching a neck, putting a soothing liquid on a foot, sending a ray of light to a shoulder, or whatever. If you see nothing at all, open your eyes for another look and then close them and try again. Be willing to try a number of times if necessary.

This meditation you may find quite difficult in the beginning. With practice, however, it can become both an important internal preparation for giving a massage as well as a good source of information about muscular tensions in the body of the person on whom you are going to work.

12

prior

This meditation, a bit more complicated than the others, can be a particularly effective last step before actually beginning a massage.

There are two ways to do it. One is to lie on your back with your arms and legs spread slightly to either side in a comfortable manner. The other is to have your friend lie in place, ready to be massaged, and actually to make contact by placing your palms lightly against his or her body.

Begin by breathing into your pelvis, as in meditation 1. Then after a little while start breathing into your right hand (remember meditation 2)? Do this for a half dozen breaths or more. Then move down to your right foot and do the same. Then the same with your left foot. And finally the same with your left hand.

Next go several times more around the same circuit — right hand, right foot, left foot, left hand — this time breathing only one breath in turn into each extremity. Then, when you feel ready, for several breaths in a row imagine sending your breath simultaneously to both hands and both feet. Try gradually to correct the "balance" of the extremities so that, as you breathe into the four of them, each is equally present in your awareness. Also, if you happen to be either standing or sitting, try to even up your sense of contact with your friend in front of you and with the ground below you.

13

This is a basic breath meditation you can use at the beginning of a massage, when your hands first start to move on your friend's body, or at any point during the massage. Essentially it is a return to meditation 1, and a continuation of the latter into the massage itself. Return to it as often as you like.

As you sit or stand, let your breath flow into your pelvis, as in meditation 1. Permit your breath to take on whatever rhythm it wishes. In particular, after each exhalation let your breath "decide" when it wants to return.

At the same time think of the movement of your hands as originating in your pelvis. Relax your shoulders as much as possible and imagine that your upper trunk, arms and hands are merely a series of extension of your pelvis. If you pay attention you will notice how each smallest movement of your hands in some way affects the position and inner sensation of your pelvis, and how each movement even affects the quality of your breathing there.

14

Here is one of the most natural steps to take after meditation 13.

Continue breathing into your pelvis, as in 13. Only now begin to imagine that with each breath cycle your exhalation travels from your pelvis to your arms and down your arms and into your hands. After a while you can even imagine that you are exhaling out your palms and into the skin and muscle of the person you are massaging. At the same time, still letting the action of your hands originate in your pelvis, think of the path of your exhalation as tracing this flow of movement in your own body.

A grounding meditation to use when doing massage at a table.

Still working with your hands as usual, begin at the same time to pay attention to your feet. Notice the pressure of the sole against the floor; and as you move your hands take in the tiny shifts that occur in the distribution of weight, and in the relation of the ankle to the foot. At the same time imagine that your breath is traveling down the leg, into the foot, and out the center of the sole.

When you feel ready move your attention to the other foot and do the same. Next try both together, breathing at once down both legs and into the floor. Then, if you want to go a step farther, try breathing into both feet and hands together. As in meditation 12, try to stay equally in contact with your friend whom you are massaging and with the floor below.

16

Another simple and effective meditation which can be used either when you first make contact with your friend's body or at any other point during the massage.

Follow your breathing without changing it for a number of breaths. Then, either by watching the movements of your friend's torso, or, with your eyes closed, letting your hands rest on his or her chest or belly or upper back, focus all your attention on your friend's breathing. Try to give yourself up totally to the rhythm and quality of his or her cycle of breath.

Most likely, as you do so, you will notice a curious phenomenon taking place. The more you give yourself up to what you are seeing or feeling, the more your own breath will begin to match the rhythm of your friend's. Allow this to happen. Then, once the breaths of the two of you feel fully synchronized, imagine that with each inhalation a single breath is filling you both. As if together you were being "breathed" by some larger power.

Another interesting means of being with your own body and with your friend's at the same time.

Whatever part of your friend's body you happen to be massaging, focus your attention also upon the corresponding part of your own body, and imagine that your hands are bringing the same relaxation and vitality to both of you at once. In other words, are you about to massage your friend's neck? Then keep aware of your own neck as you do so; as if your hands, while touching and healing your friend's flesh, had the strange capability of touching and healing your own.

18

It makes a lot of sense for a meditative approach to massage to make use of traditional healing meditations. Here is a basic one. I would suggest using it not more than once during a massage, reserving it for a part of your friend's body which for any reason seems to you as if it could use some extra attention of this sort.

Prepare yourself first with any of the other meditations. Then, when you feel ready, put your hands gently in contact with the part of your friend's body on which you have chosen to concentrate. For now have your eyes closed, and don't move your hands. Imagine that a healing energy is moving from your hands and into the body part you are touching; make use of your breathing, if you want, exhaling through your palms into your friend's body. At the same time picture to yourself the same body part as it would be if completely healthy, relaxed, and vital. Then slowly start massaging with your hands, opening your eyes now. Try to continue to hold the same image before your mind, as if your hands in their way were saying to your friend, "Look, this is how you can be."

during

19

This last is a meditation upon mortality.[1]

Keep yourself consciously aware for some minutes that the body upon which your hands are working is mortal, that it — he or she — must sooner or later die, and that in this sense right now beneath your hands is the flesh of a being who faces death. The poet Rilke says of life and death that "to affirm one without the other is a limitation which in the end shuts out all that is infinite." In the same spirit think of your own actions as a celebration: a ritual of the hands offering acceptance and praise of this inevitable death.

---

[1] A meditation you may or may not choose to explore. What it means to you will depend heavily on the present nature of your relation to your own death. If you wish to pursue this question further for yourself, see Stanley Keleman's forthcoming book on death (to be published by Random House/Bookworks).

20

This is a meditation you can use immediately after the completion of a massage.

Bring your hands to rest on your friend's body. Hold them still, applying no pressure, palms against his or her skin. Have your eyes closed. Experience your breath in your pelvis, and, as in meditation 14, imagine your exhalation going to hands.

Next, when you feel ready, slowly and gently remove your hands. Don't take them far, however. Letting them rest in the air an inch or two from the surface of your friend's body, ask yourself: what is still going on within my hands? What process, what sensations continue to take place? Especially, in what ways do you still have a sense of being in contact with your friend?

Then move some distance farther away; several feet, across the room, or wherever. Sit now, if you like, holding your hands a little in front of you. Stay with your hands. What still is going on? What degree of connection, if any, can you continue to feel between your hands and your friend's body?

This meditation is based upon a meditative exercise practiced as a part of Tai Chi Chuan. You will find it demanding, but more than worth the trouble.

Sit comfortably with your eyes closed. Rest your hands anywhere on your knees or lap. Picture to youself how you first made contact with your friend at the beginning of the massage that you have just given. Take in what you could see if your eyes were open, what sensations were in your hands, and how at the moment you experienced the rest of your body. Then slowly let yourself go over, in as much detail as possible, entire segments of the massage from beginning to end. As much as you can, try to experience the actual sequence of sensations and movements in your own body, as if some shadow of yourself were right now physically repeating the massage itself. Try also to stay fully aware of changes in emotion and feeling that arise in you.

I would suggest in the beginning that you go very slowly, and that you not try too much of this meditation at any one time. Pick out a few representative moments of the massage: perhaps, for example, a tiny bit of your work on a particular part of your friend's body. Later, if you find this meaningful for you, gradually increase the amount you choose to re-experience.

22

Another traditional healing meditation.

Sit comfortably. Stay for a while with your breathing in your pelvis. Then picture to yourself, using any image or images that come to you, a state of deep harmony between yourself and the friend whom you have just massaged. You may see the two of you dancing, or sailing together through a cloud, or whatever; stay with any single image that you like, and when you wish go on to others. Don't stop your breathing from becoming as full in your torso as it wants to.

After a short while try to expand these images in the following way. Continue to stay with images of yourself and of your friend and at the same time, as if you were drawing a bigger circle concentric to this smaller one, see if you can picture or feel another level of harmony between the two of you and the larger cosmos. Use any images, ideas, or ways of sensing your own body that fit for you. Just make sure that you imagine, if necessary as an "as if" fiction, what it might feel like directly to experience the mutual existence of yourself and your friend in the context of a larger surrounding harmony.

after

In one form or another massage has been around a long time, and hopefully will stay with us a still longer time. Hence this last meditation.

Sit comfortably, eyes closed, and as usual stay a while with your breathing in your pelvis. Then let yourself briefly go back in memory to other massages you have given (whatever ones first come to you; don't worry about remembering every last one), then to massages you have received, then to situations of learning in which you have picked up from someone else any part of what you know about massage, and finally to any occasions on which you may have passed on what you know to others in turn.

Next let all this go, and instead let yourself dwell, with whatever sense of it you find coming to you, upon the living chain, throughout history, of massages given and received, of healing through the laying on of hands and of styles and teachings handed down from individual to individual. Imagine yourself to be sensing with your body, as if you were floating in a vast sea, your own union with this tradition of touching and caring.

receiver

prior

1

A basic form of breath meditation. Essentially the same as meditation 1 of the previous section, this meditation is as excellent a preparation for receiving as it is for giving a massage.

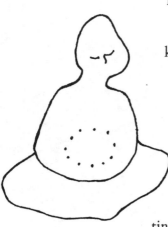

Sit comfortably. Have your eyes closed and your hands resting comfortably on your knees or lap. Turning your full attention to your breathing, follow the movement of your breath all the way down into your pelvis. Make sure that you can feel the front pelvic wall of your pelvis bulge out a tiny bit as you inhale and recede again as you exhale.

Don't try to force upon your breath any consistent rhythmic pattern. Try instead to permit its own varying rhythm to emerge from within. Especially after each exhalation try to pause until your breath itself "decides" to come back in. Give up any expectations you may have about how long this pause ought to be; it may last a fraction of a

prior

second one time, several seconds or more the next. Instead just turn the whole question over to your breath, and give all your attention to the simple texture, emotional and physical, of what you are experiencing.

As you breathe into your pelvis your breath may want also to move up into your chest. If so, by all means allow this to happen; let your ribs move gently and freely up and down. Just make sure that your attention stays with your pelvis, and that each time you inhale you can feel your breath returning there.

This simple meditation can stand by itself as a means of focusing and centering yourself before receiving a massage. Or you can use it as a "warm-up" for any of the meditations which follow.

prior

2

This meditation will help you get in touch with patterns of muscular tension in your body. The more you can make yourself consciously aware of these tensions just prior to being massaged, the more they will tend to be released by the massage itself.

Sit comfortably. Follow your breathing, as in meditation 1. Then, when you feel ready, begin to check out individual parts of your body — ankle, foreleg, knee, etc. — sensing each part from the inside and noticing, without changing anything, how tense or relaxed it feels. Work systematically through your entire body.

Next return to any single body part that felt especially tense. Each time you breathe imagine your exhalation to be flowing into this part, and at the same time try to let it relax the tiniest bit. Let each breath release the tightness just a little, as if a kind of inner warmth were slowly seeping through the muscles.

Next go in turn to two or three other of the most tense parts of yourself, and do the same. Then for a short period of time return to simply following your breathing, paying attention to the changed quality with which your breath is now flowing up and down your torso.

3

A variation of a traditional form of self-healing, think of this meditation as an inward ceremony preparing yourself to receive another's touch.

Sit. Or lie on your back. (Either will do; you can experiment and find for yourself which you prefer.) Make yourself comfortable, following your breathing as in meditation 1. Then, when you feel ready, imagine that you have found a unique and sacred spot — a groove in the woods, an underground cavern, or whatever comes to you — and have there discovered a natural spring of a liquid or balm possessing magical healing and cleansing qualities. Picture the spot, the liquid, and yourself present there as vividly as you can. Next imagine yourself, using a

51

cloth, a bowl, your hands or whatever, to be taking little bits of this liquid and gently applying it to each part of your body in turn. Take your time, make your imagining as detailed as you can; as you go to each body part try to feel against your skin the actual sensation of contact with this liquid. With each touch or stroke think of what you are doing as cleansing yourself, healing yourself, and at the same time making yourself ready for a greater wholeness to come.

4

A final simple preparation for receiving a massage.

Lie down on the massage table, or on what-ever padding has been arranged for you on the floor. Let your breath go to your pelvis, as in meditation 1. At the same time notice carefully how your body is lying on the table or padding. What parts of yourself feel in contact with the surface beneath? What parts don't? What is the exact shape of the different areas directly in contact? What, if any, surrounding areas seem also to "want" to make more contact?

Next imagine that your whole body is sinking a little lower — a shift not perceptible to the eye, but barely noticeable from within. Take your time, paying attention to the most minute events within your body: a releasing of a muscle in the neck here, a muscle in the shoulder there. At any time you feel that any particular part would like to drop even closer to the supporting surface, try lifting that part ever so slightly (it's not even necessary actually to move it as long as you mobilize the relevant muscles) and then very slowly lowering it again. Repeat this several times if you want, paying particular attention to let the part lower as fully as it wishes.

Be sure not to force or press any part

prior

downwards. Just sink. After a little while you will notice a distinct change, all up and down your body, in the way you feel yourself against the table or padding. You are ready to begin.

5

One of the simplest and best meditations while receiving a massage.

All you have to do is to focus your attention simultaneously on three easily linked parts of your experience. The first is the pressure and movement of your friend's hand. The second is the feel of the table or padding directly beneath wherever your friend is massaging you. And the third is the sheer physical or "sculptural" sensation of the portion of you that lies in between.

In other words what you are tuning into is the constantly shifting volume of your body which is being framed, above and below, by two pressures. Give your attention over to every smallest detail of what you feel within this area. Notice, for example, the varying physical distance you can feel between the hand above and the supporting surface below; any emotional stirrings — pleasure, sadness, calm, etc. — that may be here making themselves felt; the seeming tightness or flowingness, deadness or aliveness of your flesh.

During a massage return as often as you want to this meditation. You will find it new each moment, a way of being with yourself not unlike walking through an endlessly changing, endlessly fascinating piece of architecture.

6

This meditation is a variation of another traditional form of self-healing. A simple way of allowing your breath to take you deeper into the experience of being massaged, you may find it most effective after having used meditation 1 prior to the massage.

For a short while follow the movement of your breath in your pelvis as in meditation 1. Then, when you feel ready, begin with each breath to imagine that first your inhalation is entering your pelvis and then that your exhalation is flowing to that part of your body which your friend is massaging. Allow it to travel straight to your friend's hand, as if your breath could gently massage yourself from the inside while your friend is doing the same from the outside.

7

during

As I have already mentioned in *The Massage Book,* I don't normally recommend playing music during a massage: the experience tends to become a more dispersed one for both giver and receiver. Used with this meditation, however, and used sparingly, the right music can become a subtle means of deepening the effects of a massage.

The meditation itself is easy enough. At some point while you are being massaged have your friend put on the record player a piece of music which you both find agreeable. Then listen to the music and at the same time continue to follow the movements of your friend's hands: only try to sense both from *the same place.* Try, in other words, to "hear" with your leg, your shoulder, or whatever part of yourself is being massaged at the moment; let the music enter your body by mingling itself with your friend's touch.

Many deep emotions tends to be evoked in us while we are being massaged. This meditation can help you make more explicit some of your feelings about being nourished and given to by another.

Imagine yourself to be very small and young: six months or younger. You are small, helpless, your body soft and open; and you are being touched and taken care of. What feelings does this evoke in you? How does your breathing change (don't prevent it from doing so) as you let yourself take in these feelings?

Next allow yourself to "age" a little: let yourself become one year old. Does that bring about any subtle changes in the feel of your body? In your breathing?

And go on. Let yourself successively experience being two, three, and so on, right up to your present age. Only try to maintain your contact, as you move through these different ages, with that earliest sense of wonder and vulnerability in the experience of being touched. Allow this part of the child to become alive again in the body of the adult.

9

For the moments immediately after receiving a massage here is one of the easiest and best meditations I know. It can be particularly effective when you have already made use of meditation 5 during the massage itself.

Be lying on your back. Slowly go through your entire body, focusing at each point upon the inner feel of the distance between the surface of yourself lying against the table or mat and the surface of yourself directly above. Using, in other words, the same approach as that of meditation 5, let yourself make a fuller contact with whatever more articulated or more sculptural sense of yourself the massage has awakened in you.

after

10

A breath meditation that can be especially powerful soon after receiving a massage.

Be on your back. For a short while just follow your breathing, taking note of how the massage has altered the texture of your breath as you feel it moving up and down your torso.

Then, when ready, send a few breaths in turn into each of the different parts of your body. Notice the changed quality of flowingness that you will sense now in each part.

Next imagine that your breath is starting to flood through your entire body, head to toe, with each inhalation. Breathe as if the air were passing in and out the pores of your skin. Leave your mouth open, and start to take longer, larger breaths. If you don't feel too tired or wobbly, raise your knees to a point where the soles of your feet are on the ground and your legs can support their own weight. Keep your knees and feet about a foot apart.

As you breathe in this fashion, in and out through the pores of the skin, imagine that the air you are inhaling and exhaling is gradually beginning to travel greater and greater distances. Start by breathing in and out the air that lies immediately around the surface of your body. Then let the distance from which the air comes and to which it returns widen to about a foot away in all directions; then to two feet; then maybe to five or so; then twenty; and so on. After a dozen or so cycles imagine that your breath is arriving from and returning to the farthest reaches of space. Think of your breath as having become a living connection between yourself and the vastness of the cosmos.

One strong warning: don't continue this intensive form of breathing too long. Stop the moment you feel trembling, excessive dizziness, cramping, or more tingling than seems comfortable. In any case stop within five minutes. Otherwise, your body being so relaxed and open, by hyperventilating or excessively oxygenating you may charge yourself more than you are physiologically and emotionally equipped to handle.

Finish by allowing your breathing to return to its normal rate. Stay lying on your back, or, if you want, turn over on one side and curl up. As your breath gradually quiets itself, continue to think of it as seeping in and out the entire surface of your body.

after

11

When you first sit up and open your eyes, try this meditation. Or, if you feel extremely drowsy when you first get up from your massage, go get a shower, take a nap and then try this meditation when you awaken.

Be either sitting or standing. Pick out a bright color in the room and look at it. Don't try hard to focus, however; let your eyes and the muscles around them stay relaxed. Notice what, if anything, seems different or unusual about this color: its intensity, its sense of thickness or depth, its emotional quality, or whatever. Don't tighten your eyes in order to keep anything from happening. If the color wants, say, to vibrate, or to detach itself slightly from its object and float in space, or to deepen like a pool, allow this to take place.

Next go in turn through each part of your body, trying in each case to *see with that part.* For example, let your knee look as if it possessed an eye, at the same time letting the brightness of the color seep right into the knee itself. Pay attention as you do so to what you experience within yourself, to how your breathing slows or quickens, and to any ways in which the entire visual quality of the room seems slowly to transform itself.

12

This meditation is best after you have had a chance for a good rest or nap. Or try it sometime the next day, when the after-effects of your massage will still be very much with you.

Lie down and close your eyes. Choose any part of your body and, as best you can remember, go over some of the details of your friend's massaging you. Don't just "picture" what happened; try actually to experience again each successive physical sensation in your skin and muscles.

Naturally, if the massage was a good one, what you can now remember will be only the roughest of approximations. That's all right. The only important thing is to imagine as vividly as possible a sense of your friend's hand against you, and that as a minimum you make sure to cover the full surface area of the body part you have chosen.

Stop there if you wish. Or, if you like, go on to other parts of your body. For an interesting experiment, try the following.[1] Recreate the inner experience of your massage on just one side of your body: a foot, a leg, or even one entire side of yourself. Next, once you have finished, simply take

---

[1] After Moshe Feldenkrais. See his *Awareness Through Movement*, Harper & Row.

after

in the difference that you now feel between this and the opposite side of your body. Then get up, walk around, and notice the additional differences in ease and pleasantness of movement between the two sides.

both

prior

Here is a breath meditation that the two of you can use together.[1]

Sit back to back with your partner, using any comfortable cross-legged position. Move in close so that you can feel your lower spines make contact. Adjust your position so that both of you feel supported yet neither feels excessively leaned on.

Now follow your own breathing, just as in meditation 1 for the giver and meditation 1 for the receiver. Forget your partner for a moment. Allow a natural flow of breath into your pelvis, pausing slightly after each exhalation until your next inhalation decides of its own accord to return.

After a half dozen or so breaths start to focus upon your part- ner's breath as well as your own. Tune into the tiny movements that you can feel in his or her lower back. At the same time try gradually to let the

[1] After Magda Proskauer

rhythm of your own breathing come to match that of your partner's.

Since most likely one of you will have a shorter or a longer natural breath, this may require some compromise on both sides. Don't try to change everything right at once; ease slowly into a common rhythm, letting yourself take a number of breaths to get there. Try not to talk. Don't worry if you slip out of phase every now and then; just work gently back each time to the same shared breath cycle. Stay with this meditation five minutes or longer, imagining with each inhalation that you are expanding with your partner's breath as well as your own.

prior

2

A simple means of tuning more deeply into your physical contact with each other.

Sit facing your partner. Put your right palm flush against and on top of his or her left palm, and your left flush against and under his or her right. Keep your hands steady and relaxed; in contact, but not pressing hard. Have your eyes closed.

Now imagine that energy is beginning to flow between your hands and your partner's. Be patient, without trying to make anything happen. Just imagine to yourself what such a movement of energy *might* feel like.

Gradually let yourself imagine more and more of your body to be involved. Think of this energy moving up your arms, going into your chest and belly, into your neck, into your legs, etc. Don't be surprised if, after a while, you begin actually to sense a kind of current or warmth spreading through your body.

If in any part of your body you sense yourself to be particularly unreceptive, either to imagining or actually sensing something of this sort, try gently squeezing this part and letting it relax several times in succession. Then see if anything has changed.

3

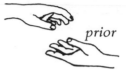

prior

A meditation much like the previous one, this time working with the feet rather than the hands.

Arrange yourself with your partner so that one of you is lying stomach down on the floor; the other is sitting, leaning back slightly, hands on the floor; the soles of your feet are touching, right against right and left against left. All eyes should be closed.

Now imagine, just as in meditation 2, that energy is beginning to circulate at the points of physical contact. Working from your feet to your ankles,

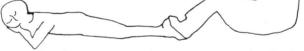

to your forelegs, to your knees, etc., gradually let more and more of yourself enter this imagined flow of energy. Without forcing, let your breathing become as open and full as it wishes. Just as in meditation 2, at any point within yourself where you feel "stuck," try gently squeezing and relaxing the surrounding muscles until you sense at least the beginnings of a difference there.

After five minutes or so of this meditation trade positions and repeat.

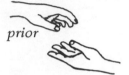

prior

4

A meditation that can both heighten your mutual receptiveness and help you each locate sources of tension in your body.

Sit or stand facing your partner. (Best to be either both sitting or both standing.) For a short while close your eyes and follow your breathing. Open your eyes when you feel ready, and, once your partner's eyes are also open, start looking up and down his or her body. Look slowly and carefully, without, however, straining or tensing your own eyes. At the same time try to feel within yourself where, if you were the tenant living inside this body before you, you might expect to experience physical tension.

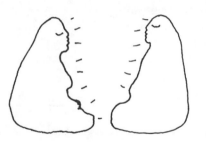

Next, reach out your hand and place your palm lightly against one of the parts of your partner's body which you have sensed as perhaps being unnecessarily tight. Don't worry about whether you are right or wrong; just follow your hunch. Let your hand rest there a couple of minutes, fully in contact but without applying

prior

pressure. Then withdraw your hand for a minute or so. Next touch your partner again in the same way, this time laying your hand on another body part from which you pick up hints of tension. And so on, touching your partner a total of anywhere from one to five or six places.

When you have finished — or before you start — let your partner go through the same process with you. While on the receiving end, simply focus your attention on the spot where your partner has laid his or her hand, and think of allowing this part of yourself to widen, to grow more spacious beneath your partner's touch.

prior

5

This last is actually a set of three meditations most effective when done together as a series.

First sit by yourself. With your eyes open hold your hands comfortably in front of you. Look at your hands for about five minutes, trying to keep them constantly in focus without glancing away. At the same time say silently to yourself, over and over, "This is me." No matter what other thoughts come to you or what unusual visual phenomena occur, keep coming back to this silent affirmation, "This is me." (The two of you can do this separately during the same time period.)

Next sit directly in front of your friend. Have him or her hold his or her hands where you can easily look at them, just as in the previous stage you looked at your own hands. Now for about the same amount of time repeat to yourself the affirmation, "This is _____ ," substituting your friend's name. (This stage must be done first by you and then by your friend. Or vice versa.)

Finally, put both your hands in direct physical contact with those of your friend. Focus now on all four hands and keep silently repeating the original affirmation, "This is me." (The two of you can of course do this at the same time.) You may let your hands gently move in relation to your friend's hands in any way you wish, as long as the

prior

four hands stay in essentially the same area and maintain physical contact.

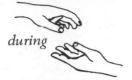

during

6

This breath meditation will enable you to continue and further develop your experience of meditation 1.

In 1 the main point was to allow the rhythmic cycle of your own breathing gradually to come to match that of your partner's. Here you do the same thing, only you follow different cues.

If you are the one giving the massage, your job is twofold. First, during each breath cycle vary the pressure of your hands so that your touch remains quite light as you inhale and then becomes noticeably stronger as you exhale. At first you may find this a little difficult to co-ordinate, but as you get into it you will find that it lends itself quite naturally to the movement of your hands. Second, watch the rise and fall of your partner's breathing, and slowly let your own breath cycle (and hence your rhythm of touch) come to match that of your partner's.

If you are receiving the massage, all you have to do is to pay attention to the pressure variations of your partner's hands (if you have a hard time tuning into this, ask your partner to make the difference more distinct), and, remembering that lightness equals inhalation and pressure equals exhalation, gradually let your own breathing come to match the rhythm that is being telegraphed to you.

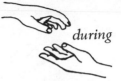

during

Whether giving or receiving, imagine, as in meditation 1, that one common breath is filling you both.

during

7

This meditation, the effects of which I find quite fascinating, is patterned after both a traditional Tai Chi Chuan meditation and the work of Moshe Feldenkrais. Although it really concerns only the experience of the receiver of the massage, because it requires the co-operation of the giver as well I include it here.

If you are the one giving the massage your role is simple. For a short time do some work, using strokes that are as clear and distinct as possible, on a part of just one side of the body. Either pick a single part that has a symmetrical counterpart — e.g., a hand or a leg — and massage it in its entirety. Or else pick, say, the torso, neck, or head, and, as if there were a vertical line running down the middle of your friend's body, thoroughly massage exactly one half. After that remove your hands from your friend's body and just wait. A little later your friend will tell you when he or she is ready to begin again.

If you are the one receiving this massage, the first thing is to pay careful attention as your friend massages a part of one side of your body. Notice the feel of the different strokes, their rhythm and timing, etc. This doesn't mean that you need to try to "picture" what an observer watching your friend might see: just take in your own experience

during

of your friend's touch as fully as you can.

When your friend has finished working on this part of you he or she will break physical contact. Go then to the opposite side of your body: to the left arm if your friend has massaged the right, to the left half of your torso if your friend has massaged the right half, etc. First just take in the difference you feel between the part that has been worked on and the part that has not. Then, using your imagination as vividly and as "physically" as possible, go in detail through the entire experience on the untouched side. Imagining, for example, that your friend is now massaging your left arm in exactly the same way as the right, try to re-create within yourself as many of these same body sensations as you can remember.

after

8

A particularly effective breath meditation after a massage is to repeat meditation 1. You will each notice a difference now both in ease of breathing and in the quality of your contact together.

9

after

Repeat meditation 2. Again pay attention to any differences you now sense in your breathing, and in the quality of the bond created between your partner's and your own hands. If you wish, you may also go on to repeat meditation 3 in the same way.

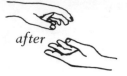
after

10

A last meditation the two of you can do together.

Sit facing your partner. Have your eyes open and look straight into your partner's eyes. Try both to keep your gaze from wandering away, and try to let any distracting thoughts pass immediately out of your mind.

After a minute or so begin to imagine that you are looking not just with your eyes, but with the entire front surface of your body. Work up to this gradually, concentrating in turn on single parts of yourself. Start with your head, imagining that your entire face is now "seeing;" then your throat, then one shoulder, and so on. Include your arms and hands and your legs and feet. Then, after you have gone through the separate parts, try "seeing" with all of them at once, as if your whole body were the living, sensitive membrane of an eye.

I would suggest not less than five and not more than fifteen minutes for this meditation. You may at some point experience flashes of hallucination. If this doesn't scare you, simply continue as before, staying open to whatever emerges before you. Take note of any images that you see, and then later, if you want, share with your partner what you observed and your feelings at this moment.

HORIZONS

Some last comments.

As you can see, especially if you have already begun to use some of the suggestions in this book, integrating meditation with massage is not difficult. On the contrary, as you may well have experienced, combining its techniques with those of massage feels like a natural flowering of meditative practice — almost as if there were something in meditation's inward build-up of intensity which of itself demanded an equivalent outward form of expression.

Which raises some questions. Look at it this way. Is it possible, as others have said, that the special strength of the East has been to develop methods of inward self-deepening and self-contact? That nevertheless the outward "translation," so to speak, of these inward forms — their complete expression in terms of transformations of the environment, of social structure, of personal relations, — remains largely unexplored territory? That precisely this stands out, for both East and West, as the task now awaiting us? And that bringing our sense of touch alive, and thereby bringing alive new depths of interpersonal contact through touch, may represent an important step towards the realization of this task?

If these questions speak to you I have three suggestions.

First, give yourself room to innovate. There are so many ways in which meditative practice lends itself to expression through massage that what I have proposed here is barely a beginning. Try out different combinations, different kinds of timing, other meditation forms, other massage styles. Do backwards what you before did forwards, then try it sideways and inside-out. Take nothing for granted and accept nothing as fixed.

Second, share with others. Whoever you are, be assured that you are not the only one on a voyage of this kind. By whatever means available to you pass on what has come to express itself in your experiences, and let yourself in turn be nourished by what has emerged for others. Granted, we cannot point to the past and speak of a "tradition" which combines meditation and massage; not in the way we can speak of meditation and certain crafts or of meditation and the martial arts. Yet traditions themselves have to start somewhere, and the way they do is by men and women sharing their discoveries, their expertise, their questionings. Look beyond yourself towards this larger context.

Finally, you can take the core of your experience through massage and meditation into the rest of your life. Here of course the guidelines are fewer. One clue which you may find helpful is that many of the meditations themselves — particularly those integrating one sense with another, or inner with outer sensation — already represent a step in this direction. Another is that the breath, so often mentioned in these pages, is a key — about which I hope to say a great deal more at a later date. Start here, patiently, and new steps and new paths will emerge for you. After all, by integrating massage with meditation what you are really teaching yourself are ways to explore with new awareness a more primordial level of your being: ways to live a little closer to that common root from which "mind" and "body" alike spring. Let yourself begin to find out for your own life what this can mean apart from all methods and techniques.

Think of yourself, and think of others exploring in the same way, as learning a new language. As having barely begun to hear its rhythm, its words, its grammar. As being like children on the brink of speech.

The Original Holistic Health Series From Random House/Bookworks:
Edited by Don Gerrard

Fine Quality Paperback Editions

George Downing, Ph.D., has taught philosophy and psychology at Yale University and Williams College, Massachusetts, and is presently a bioenergetics and gestalt therapist on the teaching staffs of Esalen Institute, The Center for Energetic Studies, and the Family Therapy Institute of Marin, in California. He is the author of *The Massage Book* and is presently completing a third work, *The Path of the Breath.*